PIANO • VOCAL • CHORD

W9-BWX-449

2005 2006 Greatest Movie Hits

Contents

Alfred

ISBN-10: 0-7390-4065-0
ISBN-13: 978-0-7390-4065-2

From the Wind-up Records release "Fantastic 4: The Album"

EVERYTHING BURNS

Words and Music by
BEN MOODY

1. She sits in her cor-ner, singin' her-self to sleep,

*All vocals written at pitch.

6

Verse 2:

2. Walk - ing____ through life un - no - ticed,

know - ing____ that no one____ cares.____

Too con - sumed____ in their mas - que - rade,____

Chorus:

AMERICA'S AVIATION HERO

(from THE AVIATOR)

Composed by
HOWARD SHORE

Moderately (♩ = 88)

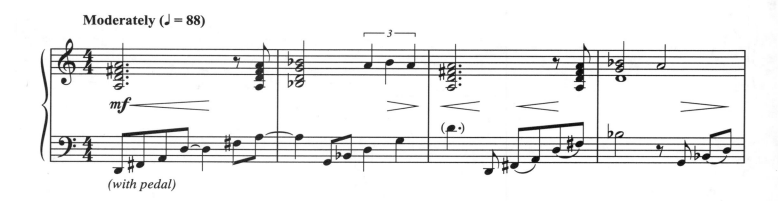

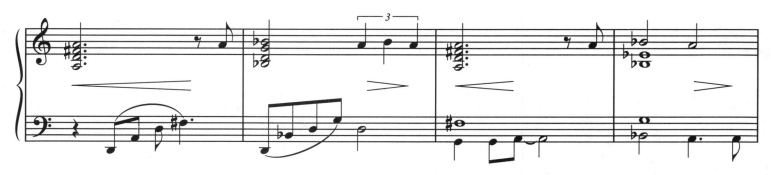

America's Aviation Hero - 2 - 1

appassionata

BATTLE OF THE HEROES

(From *Star Wars*®: Episode III Revenge of the Sith)

Music by
JOHN WILLIAMS

Maestoso, with great force (♩ = 92)

BREAKAWAY

**Words and Music by
MATTHEW GERRARD, AVRIL LAVIGNE
and BRIDGET BENENATE**

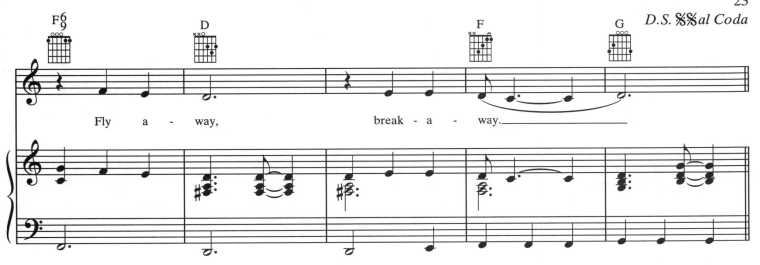

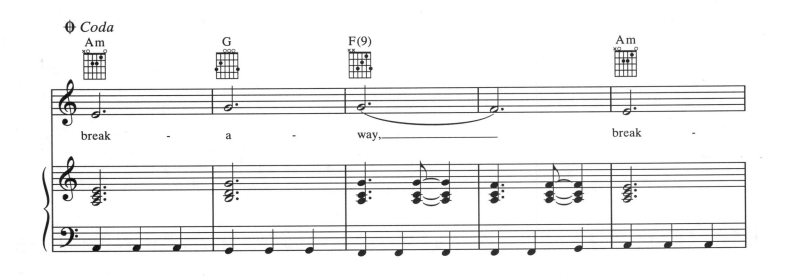

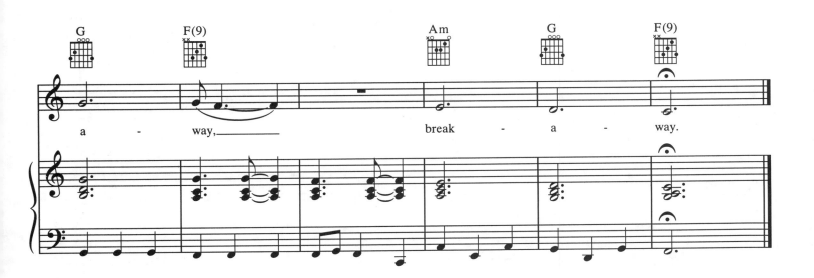

From THE POLAR EXPRESS

BELIEVE

Words and Music by
GLEN BALLARD and ALAN SILVESTRI

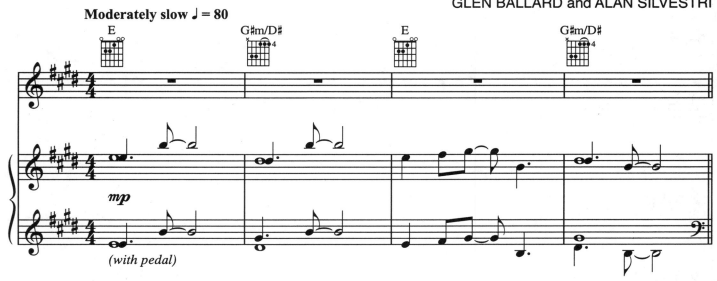

Verse:

1. Chil - dren___ sleep - ing,___ snow is soft - ly fall - ing.___
2. Trains move___ quick - ly___ to their jour - ney's end.

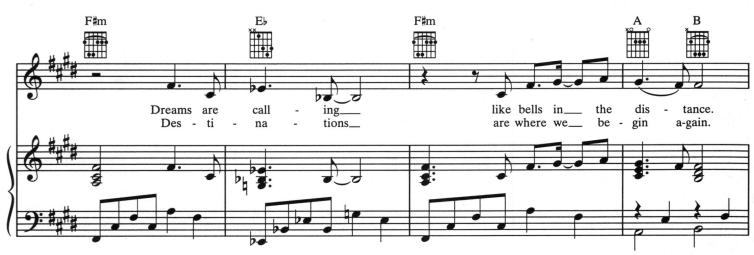

Dreams are call - ing___ like bells in___ the dis - tance.
Des - ti - na - tions___ are where we___ be - gin a - gain.

Believe - 4 - 1

BELIEVER

Words and Music by
will.i.am and John Legend

Slowly and freely ♩ = 84

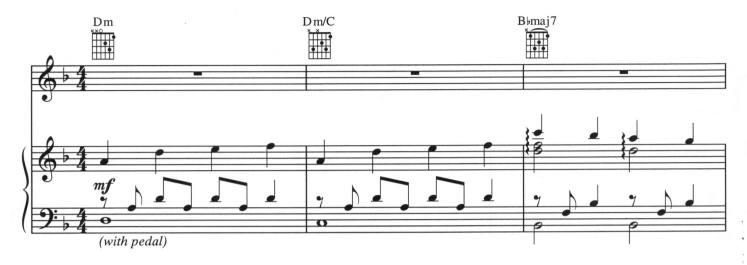

(with pedal)

Verse:

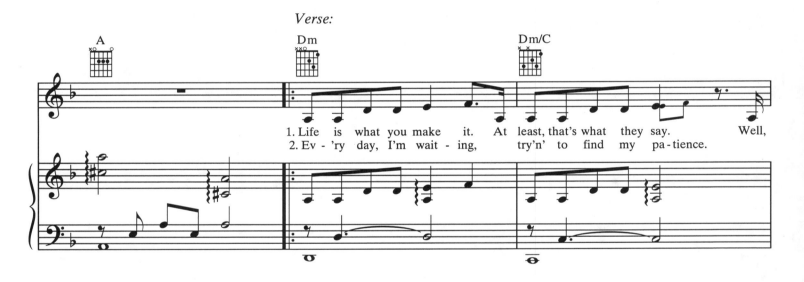

1. Life is what you make it. At least, that's what they say. Well,
2. Ev - 'ry day, I'm wait - ing, try'n' to find my pa - tience.

I think I'm gon' make it, ful - fill my dreams one day. I feel this fi - re grow - ing
So close, I can taste it, but some - times it's so hard. But I'm gon - na keep on push - ing, and

BLUE MORGAN
(from MILLION DOLLAR BABY)

Composed by
CLINT EASTWOOD

Freely and flowing (♩ = 60)

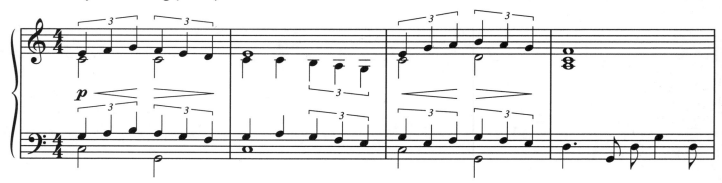

Blue Morgan - 2 - 1

CORPSE BRIDE (MAIN TITLE)

Music by
DANNY ELFMAN

Moderately ♩ = 104

(with pedal)

poco rit.

meno mosso

rit.

Slower ♩ = 84

mp

Corpse Bride (Main Title) - 3 - 1

a little faster

Moderately ♩ = 104

from BATMAN BEGINS

CORYNORHINUS
(Surveying the Ruins)

Composed by HANS FLORIAN ZIMMER,
JAMES NEWTON HOWARD, MELVYN THOMAS WESSON,
RAMIN DJAWADI and LORNE DAVID RODERICK BALFE

Moderately slow, rubato (♩ = 72)

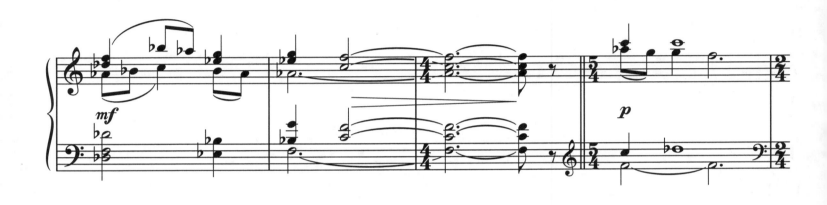

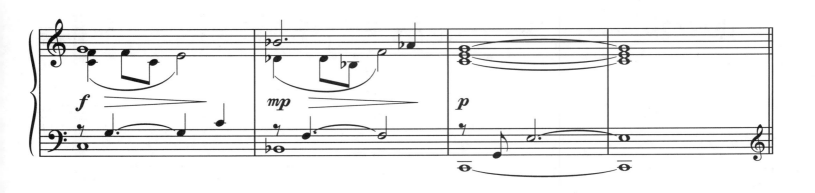

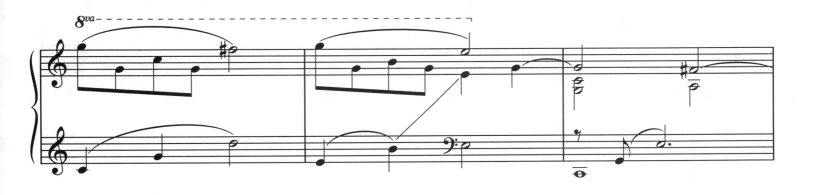

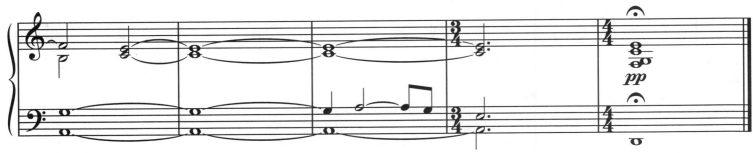

Corynorhinus (Surveying the Ruins) - 3 - 3

DO THE HIPPOGRIFF

By JARVIS COCKER and JASON BUCKLE

Bright rock ♩ = 152

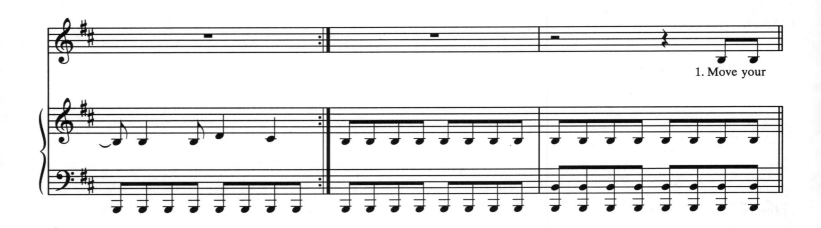

1. Move your

Verse:

bod - y like a hair - y troll,____ a - learn - ing to rock and roll.____
round_ like a scar - y ghost,____ a - spook - in' him - self the most._

From THE MOTORCYCLE DIARIES

AL OTRO LADO DEL RÍO

Letra y Música por
JORGE ABNER DREXLER

49

GOOD OL' BOYS

Moderately fast ♩ = 140

Words and Music by
WAYLON JENNINGS

Verses 1&2:

1. Just the good ol'____ boys,____ nev-er mean-in' no harm.____ Beats all____ you ev-er saw,____ been in trou-ble with the law since the day they was born.____

flat-'nin' the hills.____ Some-day the moun-tain might get 'em,____ but the law____ nev-er will.

Good Ol' Boys - 4 - 1

2. Straight-'nin' the curves,

Bridge:

Mak - in' their way,___ an - y way they know how. And that's___ just a lit - tle bit more than the law will al - low.___

To Coda

would - n't change__ if they could.

Fight-

in' the sys - tem like a true mod - ern day__ Rob - in Hood.

...end solo)

HOGWARTS' HYMN

By PATRICK DOYLE

Nobilmente con expressivo (♩ = 69)

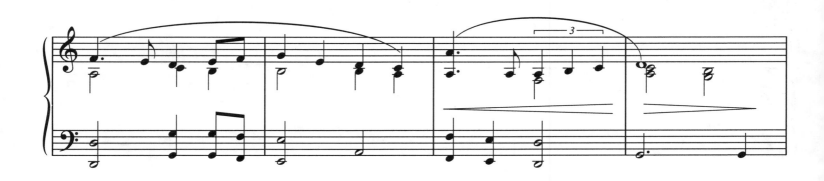

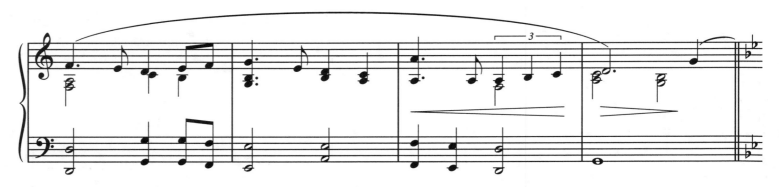

Hogwart's Hymn - 3 - 1

Hogwart's Hymn - 3 - 2

Opening Theme from

MARCH OF THE PENGUINS

(The Harshest Place on Earth)

Composed by
ALEX WURMAN

March of the Penguins - 3 - 1

a tempo

March of the Penguins - 3 - 3

MAGIC WORKS

By JARVIS COCKER

Spoken: This one's going out to all the lovers out there.

(with pedal)

Hold each other tight, and keep each other warm.

1. And

Verse:

dance
make

your fi - nal___ dance.___
your fi - nal___ move,___

Magic Works - 4 - 1

STAR WARS
(Main Title)
(From *Star Wars*®: Episode III Revenge of the Sith)

Music by
JOHN WILLIAMS

Majestically, steady march (♩ = 108)

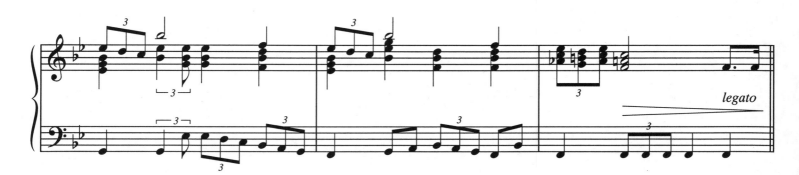

Star Wars - 4 - 1

66

Star Wars - 4 - 4

THIS IS THE NIGHT

By JARVIS COCKER

Moderately slow ♩ = 76

When all is dark and there's no light,

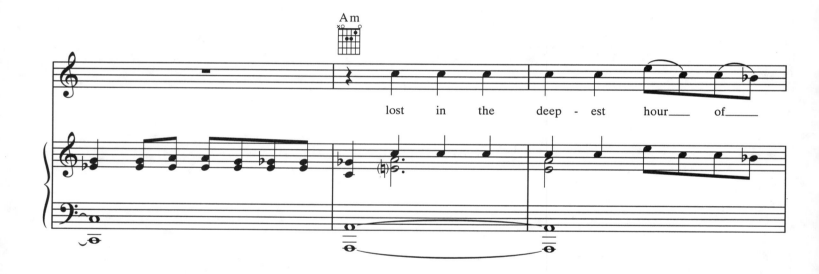

lost in the deep-est hour of

night, I see you.

This Is the Night - 6 - 1

Chorus:

So take you hands off me to - night. I'm break - ing free. This is the night.

This is the night.

So take your hands off me to -

night. I'm break-ing free. This is the night.

1.

This is the night.

2.

This is the night.

This is the night.

Verse 2:
There was a time I would have walked on burning coals for you,
Sailed across the ocean blue,
Climbed the highest mountain just to call your name.
The moon throws down its light and cuts me to the quick tonight.
A change is in the air and nothing will ever be the same.
You still look good to me,
Ooh, but you're no good for me.
I close my eyes and squeeze you from my consciousness.
And in the morning when I wake,
I walk the line, I walk it straight,
But the morning's so many miles away.
Good God now!
(To Chorus:)

From Warner Bros. Pictures' CORPSE BRIDE

VICTOR'S PIANO SOLO

Music by
DANNY ELFMAN

Victor's Piano Solo - 2 - 1

*F✕ = G♮

WONKA'S WELCOME SONG

Music by DANNY ELFMAN
Lyrics by JOHN AUGUST and DANNY ELFMAN

Wil - ly

Won - ka, Wil - ly Won - ka, the a - maz - ing choc - 'la - tier. Wil - ly

Won - ka, Wil - ly Won - ka, ev - 'ry - bod - y give a cheer! He's

Wonka's Welcome Song - 4 - 1

78

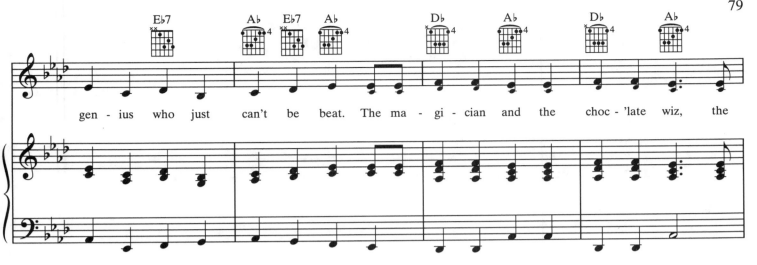

gen - ius who just can't be beat. The ma - gi - cian and the choc - 'late wiz, the

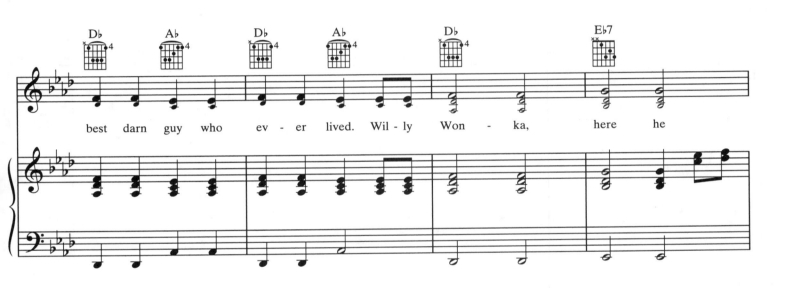

best darn guy who ev - er lived. Wil - ly Won - ka, here he

is!

From Warner Bros. Pictures' CORPSE BRIDE

REMAINS OF THE DAY

Additional Lyrics by
JOHN AUGUST

Music and Lyrics by
DANNY ELFMAN

Moderately ♩ = 92

Bridge:

con-jured up a plan to meet late at night. They told not a soul, kept the whole thing tight. Now her

moth-er's wed-ding dress fit like a glove. You don't need much when you're real-ly in love, ex-

cept for a few things, or so I'm told, like the fam - i - ly jewels and a satch-el of gold. Then

next to the grave-yard by the old oak tree, on a dark fog-gy night at a quar-ter to three, she was

Chorus:

Everybody:

bride.

Die, die, we all___ pass a - way,___ but don't wear a frown___ 'cause it's

___real - ly o - kay.___ You might try and hide,___ and you might try and pray,___ but we

You might try and pray,___ but we

all end up the re - mains *ad lib.*   *Yeah!*

all end up the re - mains of the day.